The Complete Do-It-Yourself Solar Panel Guide

This book was written with the goal of helping people make their own solar panels. Designed to help both the beginner and advanced solar panel builder, it is sure to have something for everyone.

This is the compilation of the results of three years intensive research and experiments to provide the most comprehensive book possible.

With energy costs rising, and the price of solar technology decreasing, more and more people are turning to solar energy for their homes.

Here at the Do-It-Yourself World we have the aim of helping people save on their energy bills, while becoming a little bit self reliant.

The Complete Do-It-Yourself Solar Panel Guide

Lulu ISBN 978-1-105-34967-6

Special thanks go to my sister, Danielle Reid, for her dedication and hard work as an editor.

Contents

The Complete DIY Solar Panel Guide

First of all, I believe that a photo really does speak a thousand words. Therefore I use a lot of photos in this instructional book to give a very clear understanding of how each and every step is accomplished. The main idea is to keep everything as simple as possible so that anyone who has a bit of mechanical skills can make their own solar panel with ease.

This book is a compilation of 20 years of experimentation with solar energy and 3 full years of intensive research and testing various solar cell configurations. This project was started three years ago and was supposed to be finished within a few months. After some trial and error, and much failure, I decided to wait until further testing was completed in order to provide the most comprehensive DIY solar panel book possible.

In this book, I discuss the best and worst materials that can be used to construct a solar panel. It will not only cover how to prepare each solar cell for soldering, but also how to solder the tabbing wire to the solar cells and how to string them together to make a solar panel.

There is a section on what materials to use to make a frame for your solar panel. And, finally, how to hook up the solar panel to a battery bank, charge controller and power inverter to run appliances in your home.

The intentions of this book are to give a simple, easy-to-follow guide to make your first solar panel from scratch, using materials that are affordable and easy to work with. There may be better materials for long term solar panel life, such as metal framing instead of wood, but then it will not be a DIY book for everyone on a budget. Also, some people cannot work with metal as well. Not only is wood a simpler base, but most lumber yards will cut it for you, normally for free. Both materials will be covered, though, so you have a choice, if money and metal working are not an issue.

Please feel free to swap out materials suggested in this book for those that you have on hand already. Remember, this is just a guideline. For example, plexiglass is suggested for a cover on the solar panel due to its ease of use, but if your preference is for real solar glass, then you are welcome to substitute it.

You may, or may not, buy solar cells that come pre-tabbed, which means that the tabbing wire is already in place. This saves you a lot of time and trouble soldering. This book details starting from just the plain solar cells, delivered to you in bulk from a dealer.

It is also your option to use broken solar cells instead of whole ones. The only difference with broken solar cells is to make sure to get good connections on both the positive and negative sides of the cells when soldering.

Solar panels can deliver nearly full power output with little or no maintenance for 20 years or more.

It is possible to make your own solar panels for under a dollar per watt. By using broken or lower grade solar cells, and buying in bulk, you can lower the total cost. Also, you can use cheaper framing materials such as wood instead of metal or plastic. Use plexiglass instead of solar glass. All methods are covered here.

Note: If you already understand the basics of solar panels and what parts you need, please feel free to skip ahead to "Part One – Getting Started".

8

Solar Panel Basics – An Introduction To Solar Panels

About Solar Panels

Put simply, solar panels convert the energy from the sun directly into usable electricity. That electricity is normally stored in a battery bank for later use. Otherwise, if you did not store the energy, at night you would not have any usable energy available. No sunlight equals no energy produced.

A solar panel generally puts out 18 Volts in full sunlight. This will be converted by a Solar Charge Controller, which will be covered later.

A solar panel is made up of individual solar cells. These solar cells are then connected to get the desired voltage and power output. Most solar cells put out about 0.5 volts or 1 volt. They are rated with the amount of Amps that they put out in full sunlight.

In the example used later in this book, there is a series of solar cells that put out 0.5 Volts each. You need a total of 18 Volts for a solar panel, so 36 solar cells are used to get the 18 volts. 36 x 0.5 = 18.

The solar cells in the example put out 3.75 Amps of energy. The finished solar panel will put out a total of 3.75 Amps of usable energy for each hour that the sun is shining.

In calculating solar power requirements, you can use Amps or Watts, depending on how the device you are using is rated. A light bulb, for example, is rated in Watts. A 100 Watt light bulb uses 100 Watts of energy per hour that it is running. This energy consumption is rated in Watt Hours or WH, so our light bulb uses 100 WH every hour that it is turned on.

An electric motor, such as a power drill, is normally rated in Amps. Let's say you are using a power drill rated at 5 Amps. If you run the power drill for an hour, you are using 5 Amps per Hour. This is called Amp Hours or AH. Our power drill uses 5 AH.

Watts is a total of Volts multiplied by Amps, so the example solar panel setup will put out 18 Volts times 3.75 Amps = 67.5 Watts of usable energy per hour.

All of these calculations become important when figuring out the total power that you need from your solar panel setup. Do not let these numbers confuse you. This subject will be discussed again.

About Power Inverters

The next step is to convert the 12 Volt stored energy from the batteries into 120 Volts for normal household appliances. This is done with a power inverter. A power inverter usually has a cigarette lighter plug on one end and a 120 Volt socket on the other. They can be found in most gas stations, automotive shops or RV stores.

Another type of inverter is a grid tie inverter. These allow solar energy output to be tied directly into the electrical grid. This allows us to sell extra, unused energy back to the power companies. The grid tie inverter is beyond the scope of this DIY introduction book, so we will stick to the common automotive inverter. Due to safety regulations in most states, if you do want to go that route you will have to pay a professional to hook it up for you.

A common automotive power inverter

In the photo above, you can see a common automotive inverter.

This one is rated at 175 Watts continuous and 350 Watt peak. You want to use the continuous rating when choosing an inverter.

The peak rating is what the inverter can handle for a short, quick time; such as starting a motor, which consumes a large amount of power for a second or two while it starts up.

An Introduction To Lead Acid Batteries

Lead acid batteries – the same used in a car – are just about the same thing as a marine, or deep cycle battery. The main difference is that a car battery is built to be able to put out a huge amount of power in an instant in order to start your car. A deep cycle battery, on the other hand, is designed to put out a fair amount of power over a long period of time.

A lead acid battery (simplified) is composed of lead plates suspended in an acid. This arrangement allows a large amount of energy to be stored chemically in the battery. Due to their large storage capacity, lead acid batteries are perfect for solar power use. During the daylight hours, the solar panels charge up the batteries. At night you can use this stored power for lighting your house, or running a computer or television.

For solar power projects, it's preferable to use a deep cycle or marine battery. You do not want a dual purpose starting battery / deep cycle battery. If you already have one lying around, it can be used. If, instead, you are buying a battery for this project, then choose a deep cycle only battery.

The reason for the above mentioned preference is that a dual purpose battery is designed to be able to start a boat motor as well as provide a large amount of energy during a long period of time. Starting batteries will generally have a shorter life span and cannot provide as much long term output energy as a pure deep cycle battery can.

Golf cart batteries are often used due to their rugged build, large capacity and relatively low price. Most golf cart batteries are 6 volts, so they are often connected together in series to get 12 volts.

A deep cycle battery is normally rated in AH, or Amp Hours. This means that if the battery is rated at 100 AH, then it can provide 1 Amp for 100 hours, or it can provide 20 Amps for 5 hours. Simply divide the total AH rating of the battery by the number of Amps you will be using, and you will get the number of hours this battery will provide power. This calculation is not perfect, but it is a general guideline when choosing a battery.

Starting batteries are rated in CA, which means Cranking Amps. If you see this rating on a battery, avoid it, if possible. It may work for you, but will not have as much capacity as a pure deep cycle battery. An example is a battery with 600 CCA. This means it can provide 600 Amps of power to start your car in cold weather.

Some deep cycle batteries may be rated with RC, or Reserve Capacity. This is the number of minutes a battery can maintain a useful voltage at 25 Amps. A battery rated at 160 RC, for example, can handle a drain of 25 Amps for 160 minutes.

You can convert RC (Reserve Capacity) to AH (Amp Hours) for your project. In the example above, we have a battery with 160 minutes reserve capacity. Divide the minutes by 60 to get hours. In this example, we have 160 / 60. We get a total of 2.67 hours. Now multiply this by 25 to get the total Amp Hours capacity of this battery. With our example, we get 2.67 x 25 = 66.7 AH.

The battery above then, rated at 160 Reserve Capacity (RC), is roughly equal to a 66.7 AH (Amp Hour) battery. This is a rough calculation, but sufficient for our purposes here.

For the remainder of this book, we will be using AH, Amp Hours for our battery ratings because it is more commonly found.

A standard 12 Volt battery is usually charged by a voltage of between 13 to 15 volts. A lead acid battery is normally considered full when its voltage is between 12.6 to 12.8 Volts.

Never discharge a battery below 10.5 Volts, or it will be permanently ruined. Most power inverters have an automatic cut off switch inside to prevent this from happening. Some inverters simply have an alarm that sounds when the voltage gets too low to warn you. When choosing an inverter, choose one that shuts itself off automatically to prevent battery damage if you are not around to monitor it.

Generally you will try to keep your battery above 11.5 volts for longer life. Every battery will eventually wear out, but by keeping a battery within its comfortable operating limits, it will last much longer.

Do not worry; you will be using a Solar Charge Controller for this project. In this way, your battery's charge state will be automatically adjusted and maintained for you.

A solar charge controller takes the 18 volts output by a solar panel and converts it to the 12 volts needed by the battery. The charge controller monitors the battery voltage and will shut off the load (your light or television, for example) when the voltage drops too low. It will also make sure that the battery does not get overcharged by the solar panels by disconnecting them at full charge. The solar charge controller is designed to provide optimum battery life and service by maintaining the proper charge and discharge voltages automatically.

A battery bank is a set of two or more batteries wired together to increase the total usable power output. For example, you may have two batteries rated at 100 Amp Hours and want to connect them together to get a total of 200 Amp Hours. You can do this by connecting them together in parallel. This means that you connect both positive outputs together and then connect both negative outputs together. Now you have a battery bank of 200 AH capacity. You can run a load of 200 Amps for one hour or 1 Amp for 200 hours, or anything in between.

Battery banks are normally 12 Volt, but can also be 6-, 24-, or 48 Volt or even more. For simplicity, we will use a standard 12 Volt battery bank for our solar panel setup.

Batteries also have what is called a C20 Rating. The C20 rating is a calculation of how many amps a battery can put out over a 20 hour period. For example, a 100Ah battery has a C20 rating of 5 Amps. 100 Ah divided by 20 hours = 5 Amps. This battery can sustain a drain of 5 Amps for 20 hours. This is considered the safest current drain for your battery. Drawing more current repeatedly can damage the battery.

Warning: Lead acid batteries are capable of putting out tremendous amounts of energy in a split second. They are capable of melting wires and metal. Fire or personal harm can occur if you do not handle lead acid batteries with respect.

Also, lead acid batteries do contain acid. This acid will burn the skin and instantly eat holes in clothing. Keep baking soda around in case any acid comes out of the top of the battery. This will neutralize the acid and render it harmless. Wear old clothes or an apron when working with batteries.

Lead acid batteries give off hydrogen gas while being charged. They must be vented to the outside in order to prevent the risk of an explosion.

How to choose the right equipment for your needs

Note: The following information is copied directly from our website: http://www.thediyworld.com/The_Solar_Panel_Requirements_Calculator.html

For simplicity, let's assume you have a 100 watt device (light bulb – for example) that you want to power with free solar energy for 10 hours each night. To figure out what size solar panel, batteries, charge controller and inverter you need, follow the simple steps below.

1. Calculate how much energy is needed in Watt Hours. Multiply your Watts needed by the number of hours you will use the device:

100 Watts x 10 hours = 1,000 Watt hours. That is the total energy you will need in Watt Hours.

2. Now calculate what size solar panel you will need. Divide your total number of Watt Hours needed by the total number of sunlight hours available. Use your total Watt Hours requirement of 1,000. Based on an average ten hour day of light, the calculation is simple:

1,000 Watt hours / 10 hours sunlight = 100 Watt solar panel.

The reality is that most summer days give about 15 hours of sunlight, and in winter (up north) you get about 4-5 hours of sunlight. Always choose the worst case scenario for your solar panel. In this case, go with a winter day of 5 hours sunlight. (Based on average United States daily sunlight hours.)

1,000 Watt Hours / 5 hours sunlight = 200 Watt solar panel.

3. Calculate what size batteries you need in Amp Hours. Divide your total number of Watt Hours needed by the battery voltage. Use your total requirements of 1,000 Watt Hours and a battery voltage of 12 Volts. 1,000 Watt Hours divided by 12 Volts = 83 Amp Hours of reserve battery power.

1,000 / 12 = 83.3

An average marine deep cycle battery will work well here. Select a larger size battery to be sure, say 100 Amp hours capacity.

4. To figure what size solar charge controller is needed, take your solar panel wattage, which is 100 watts divided by 12 Volts.

100 / 12 = 8.3 Amps.

Always go larger. In this case, use a 10 Amp solar charge controller.

5. Calculate what size inverter is needed. That's the easy part. You need to power a 100 Watt load, so select an inverter that has at least 100 Watts continuous power rating.

Note: If you live in sunny, warmer climates, please adjust your calculations appropriately.

Note: If you need help calculating your solar power needs, please use our free online solar power calculator:

http://www.thediyworld.com/The_Solar_Panel_Requirements_Calculator.html

Part One of the Project – Getting Started

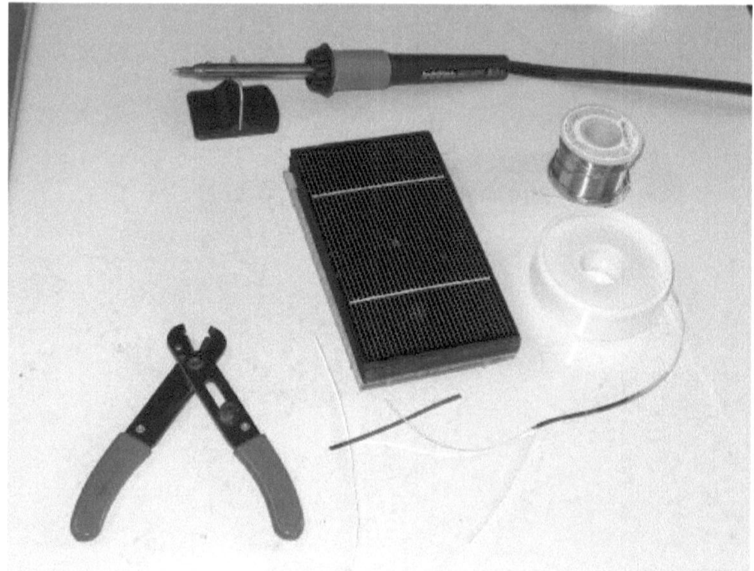

Tools you will need.

For this project, you will need:

- your solar cells
- a very good soldering iron
- a spool of fine solder
- some tabbing wire
- a pair of wire cutters.

The tools can be purchased at your local Radio Shack or hardware store. It is a good idea to spend a bit more on the soldering iron because it is the most important tool in this project. A soldering iron slowly burns off its tip, and a cheap iron will lose it more quickly than a good one.

Get a spool of fine rosin core solder. You will be doing some fine work here, so smaller diameter solder is better. The solar cells can be found on the internet relatively inexpensively. Those acquired for this project, along with 100ft of fine tabbing wire, were from an online store.

Another suggestion is to keep a damp sponge nearby to clean off the tip of your soldering iron each time you set it down. Otherwise it will burn off its tip faster. Visit our website www.thediyworld.com for more details about soldering and info on how to get the beginners guide to soldering, if needed.

Warning: solar cells are extremely fragile! They are very thin and break relatively easy. Be careful and handle them gently.

Begin Solar Panel Assembly

Start out by measuring your solar cells and making a layout for your solar panel. The recommended voltage for a solar panel is 18 Volts.

The solar cells in this example are rated at 0.5 volt per cell and 3.75 Watts each. So, simple math: 0.5 x 36 = 18 volts, gives me 36 solar cells to make up one complete solar panel. Yours may vary depending on the specifications of your particular cells. Just keep it simple and try to get a total of 18 volts.

Two solar panels, each with 18 solar cells, were used in order to keep the size of the panels down a bit. See the diagram below for solar cell placement The arrows represent the electrical connection in series between all the cells.

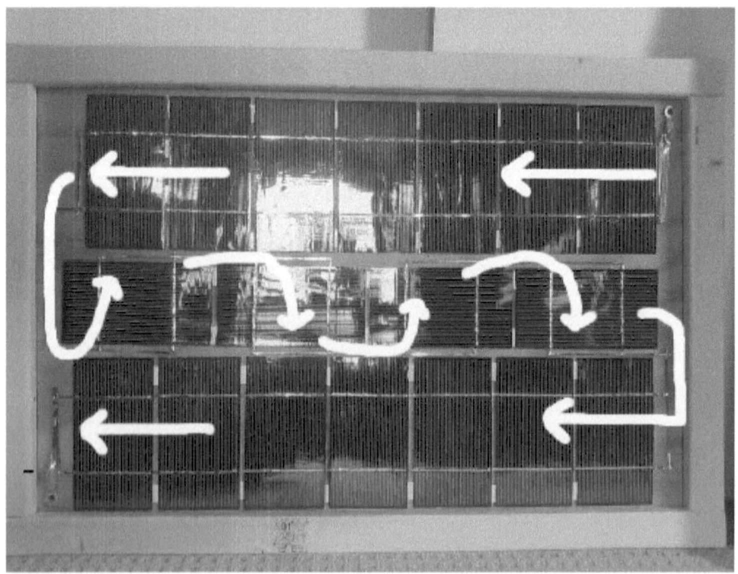

The deciding factor on this particular solar panel design was based on the available plywood. There were two pieces at 19 inches by 29 inches lying around. This fits perfectly for the two panels using the pattern as developed and shown in the previous photo.

The main point is that the cells are all connected in series. That means that the plus of one cell feeds into the minus of the next, and so on.

What you will have is a long series of solar cells + - + - + - + - + - + - with one end being the positive terminal, and the other end being the negative terminal. It does not really matter how you set up your solar panel as long as all of the cells are in series as shown above and in the next image.

Your own project will vary based on the physical dimensions of the solar cells you get and the available materials that you will use to make your panel. Also, you may be using broken or chipped solar cells. In this case, the layout is the same as below.

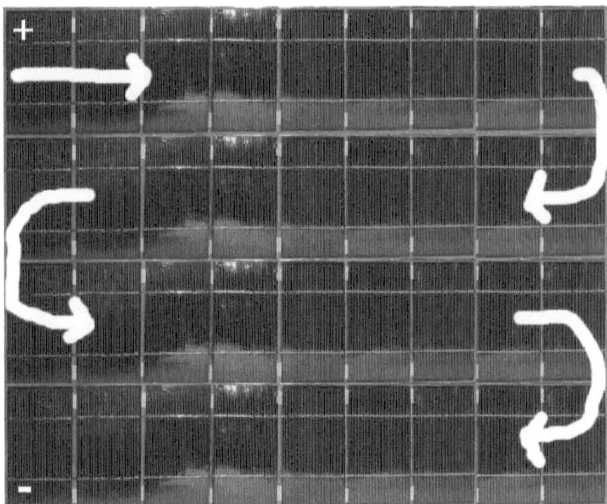

In the image above, you can see a standard solar panel layout using 3x6 inch solar cells. There are a total of 36 solar cells soldered together in series to make an 18 volt solar panel. If materials are not a determining factor in your design, then use a simple layout such as the one above. There are 4 rows of 9 solar cells connected together in series. The arrows show the connection of the bus bars between each row.

If you are using 6x6 inch solar cells, then you can use 6 rows of 6 solar cells, giving you a 36 inch square solar panel in the end.

Again, you are not constrained to any set pattern, as long as the solar cells are all connected in series.

Note: Since this is a DIY project on a budget, you may be using materials that can be found lying around to keep the price down. If no other factors are involved, such as being limited by the size of available materials, use a standard layout such as suggested above.

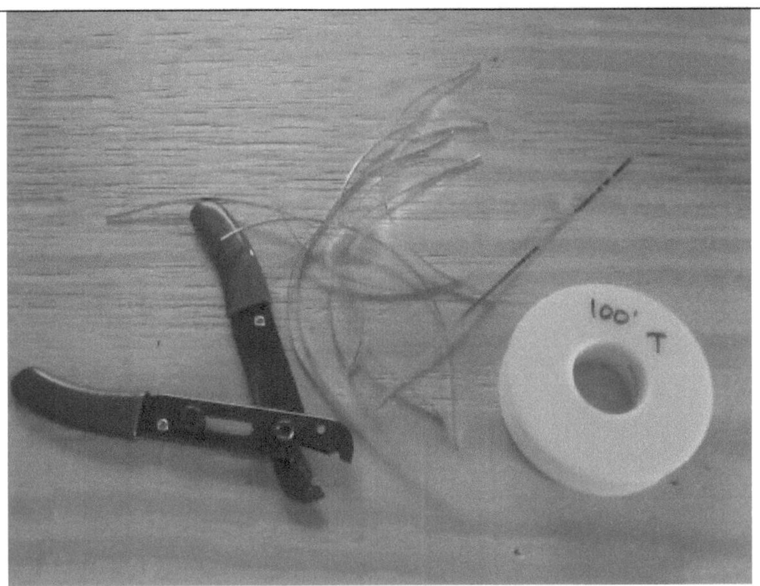

Cut the tabbing wire.

Now cut the tabbing wire. You will need 2 pieces of tabbing wire per solar cell. Cut the wire just a little bit shy of twice the length of a solar cell. The tabbing wire must go from the top of one solar cell to the bottom of the next one.

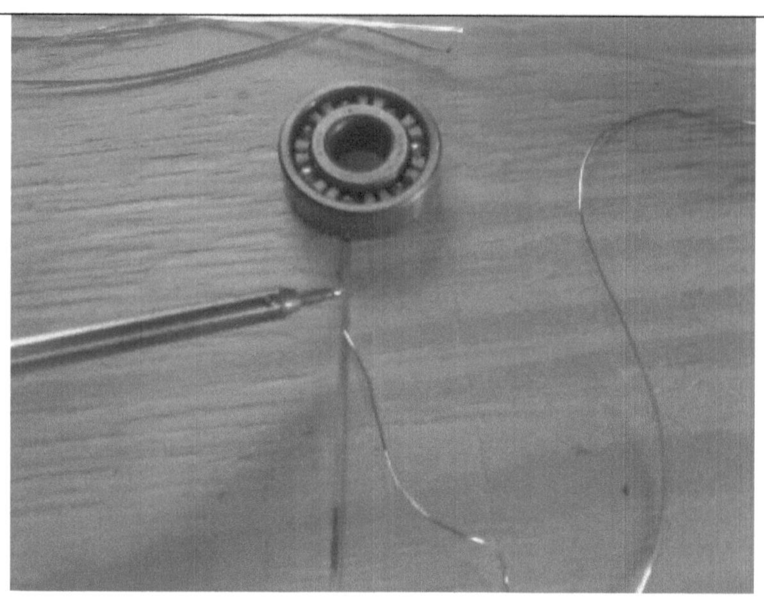

Pre-tin the tabbing wire strips.

Next, pre-tin the tabbing wire so that it will stick better to the cells later on. As seen in the photo, an old piece of metal was used as a weight to hold the piece of wire down while soldering. Using a piece of wood as a back drop to the work space protects the desk top. Soldering is a bit messy and the rosin tends to get burnt into your work surface.

Run the iron quickly down the length of each wire, feeding the solder into it as you go. Do this for all of your wire pieces. This step is not very critical and can go quickly. The tabbing wire accepts solder very easily.

Pre-tin the top of solar cells.

Now, carefully pre-tin the top terminals of each solar cell. Run the soldering iron slowly along the silver band on top of the solar cell, feeding solder continuously just under the tip of the soldering iron. You do not need to apply pressure to the solar cell. The heat from your soldering iron does the work. When you are finished, it should look like the photos at the right and below. Try not to stay on one point too long or you may damage the cell.

Try to get a smooth, perfect bead of solder along the whole strip. Repeat this step for all of your solar cells and carefully set them aside as you go.

Note: It is alright to stop for a second and come back if you get stuck.

The board used for a work surface helped a lot to keep the solar cells from sliding all over the table.

View of the pre-tinned top of a solar cell.

Solder the tabbing wire onto the top of the solar cell.

Again the little metal weight comes in handy for the next step. Use something to anchor one of the tabbing wires down while you work. Align the wire directly over one of the top terminals of the solar cell. Slowly run the soldering iron over the top of it, while feeding solder continuously just under the tip of the iron as you go. Use the solder sparingly. You do not need much because you already tinned both surfaces.

This step simply insures a good connection between the two surfaces. Repeat this step for all of your solar cells and carefully set each one aside, away from your work area.

Note: Be very careful not to push too hard on the surface of the cell, or it may break.

Try not to linger too long on any single point. Remember, it is alright to stop for a second if you get hung up.

A cheap soldering iron will often need a couple seconds pause to heat back up while you are working. Sometimes the solder wire may stick to the cell without melting at one point. In this case, remove the soldering iron for a second, and allow it to reheat. Touch the solder while gently pulling away to remove it from the cell and continue where you left off.

Tabbing wire is soldered onto top of solar cell.

The top side of one solar cell is finished.

The top photo on the previous page shows one of the tabbing wires in place on top of the solar cell. The photo below it shows both of the top terminals with their tabbing wires in place.

Bottom of a solar cell.

When you have all of the top terminals soldered, you can take one of the solar cells and turn it upside down as shown.

Start soldering the bottom tabs on the solar cell.

Put a bit of solder on each of the square terminal points on the bottom of the cell.

Using a gentle side-to-side sliding motion over the contact while feeding a bit of solder under the tip of the soldering iron works best.

Soldering the bottom tabs of the solar cell.

Bottom tabs are pre-tinned.

Now do the same for all of your cells, until they all look like this.

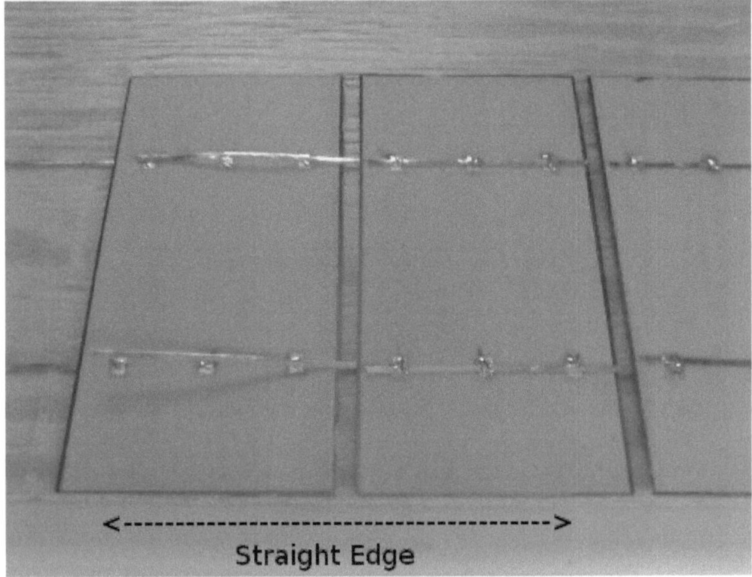

Solder the cells together.

At this point you are ready to start connecting all of the solar cells together.

Use the board edge (your work surface mentioned earlier) as your guide to help align all of your cells in a straight row.

First, lay out two of your tabbed solar cells on the table top, aligning the bottom edges of your cells to the edge of your work surface, as shown.

Solder the tabbing wire from the top of the first solar cell to the bottom of the next cell. Do this as previously described, connecting all your cells in series. Whereas the example plans called for seven cells together in each row, your design may vary.

Note: It helps to use a small weight to keep the tabbing wire in place and in contact with the surface of the solar cell while doing this step. Be very careful if you do this!!! The solar cells are very fragile and can easily be broken.

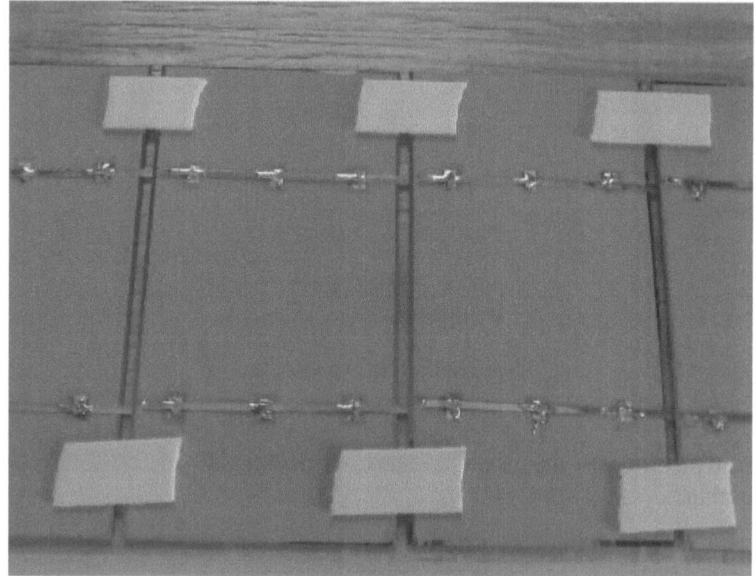

Tape cells together for strength.

Handling your new row of solar cells can be very tricky without helping hands. In the photo, little strips of double sided tape were used to hold them all together a bit more stiffly and help when moving them around.

Scotch tape is better for this step. It is thinner and easier to work with.

Note: At this point, there are three sets of solar cells. They will not be connected together at this stage. Depending on your layout, you may now have 4 or 6 sets of solar cells.

Part two of the project – make the frame

Note: The following assumes a budget solar panel assembly. You may use metal or plastic instead of wood for the following steps.

At this time, put aside all the solar cells for a while. This next step assumes some bit of mechanical skills working with wood. You will need to get some marine grade plywood, some trim from the local hardware store, some small screws and two sheets of plexiglass.

It is best if you go to a place like Home Depot and have them cut the wood and plexiglass for you. Otherwise, get a saw out and prepare for some cutting.

For this project, two pieces of 8 ft long wooden trim were purchased for a dollar each to make the frame. This is to give a bit of a gap between the solar cells and the protective plexiglass cover.

You will need a hand saw or table saw, drill and bits, screwdriver, tape measure, pencil and some “C” clamps for this part.

Simply cut your plywood backboard to the proper dimensions. For this project, there were a couple pieces, measuring 19 x 29 inches, laying around that fit perfectly. That was then the main deciding factor in the layout of the solar cells for this project.

Notes: Use marine grade plywood, if possible. If you use normal plywood, then paint all surfaces heavily and use silicon to seal all cracks and seams.

As you may notice in the next few photos, it is not necessary to paint all parts ahead of time. You may decide to assemble all the frame parts first, then paint it all together. It is highly recommended to paint everything thoroughly and caulk every crack to protect your panels.

Paint the wood.

Tools and parts required.

Laying out the tools needed.

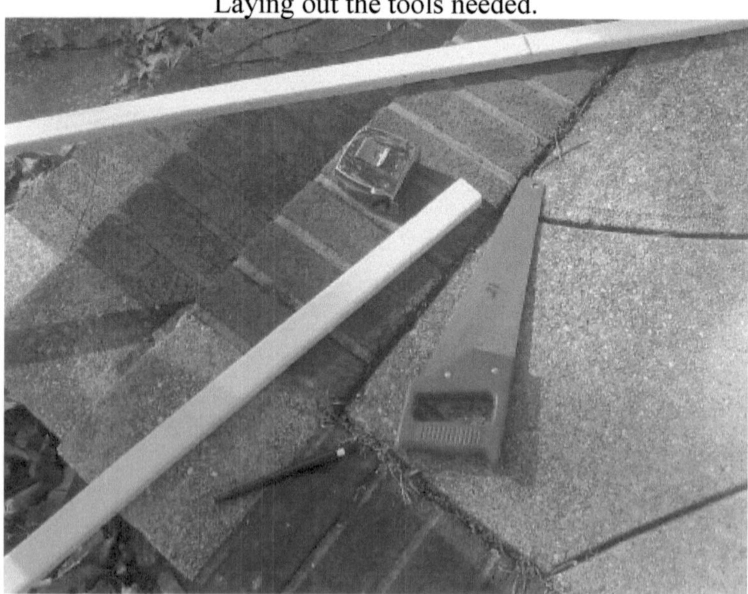

To make things simple, basic tools were used for these examples. In the previous photo, some of the wood pieces have already been cut. Four pieces were cut at 29" and fastened, two each, to the long sides of the plywood back boards. After measuring how much space was left in between the ends of those pieces, the other four pieces were cut – top and bottom parts.

Please read through the following steps first to get an idea.

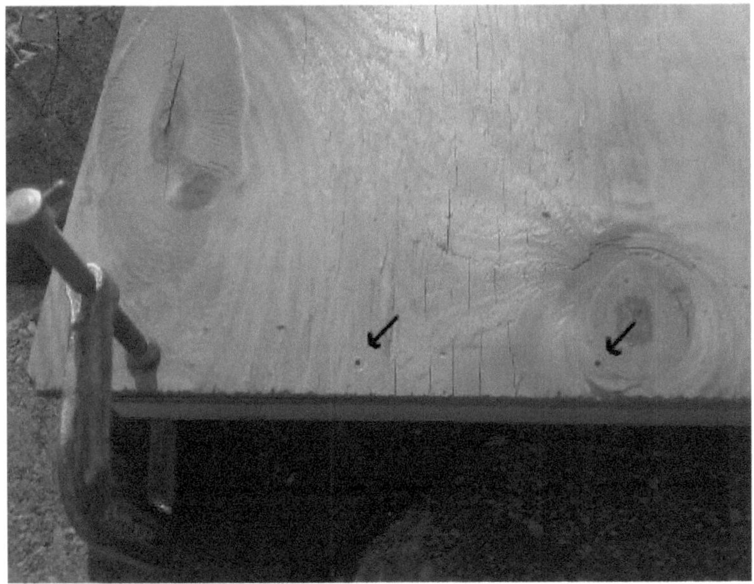

Pre-drill holes.

Using a "C" clamp to hold the wooden trim pieces in place, drill through the plywood, just enough to give the screws a good grip for the next step. A drill bit that is just a little smaller than the screws makes them go in easier, while allowing them to grip well. This will help keep the wood from splitting when you insert the screws.

See above photo.

Next, attach the frame pieces with screws through the previously drilled holes. See the photo below. The arrows show individual screws through the wood backing and into the frame.

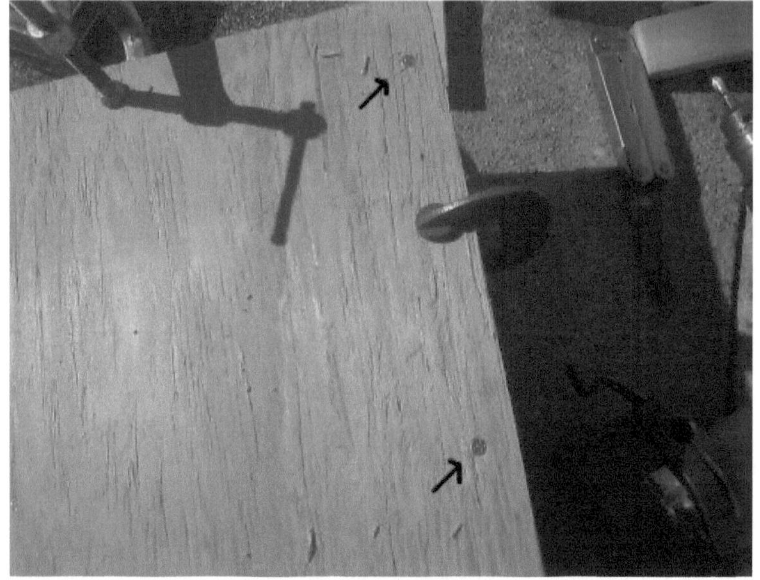

Screw parts together.

In the photo below, you see the completed frame for the solar panel.

Finished Frame.

Depending on your layout and plan, you may have a single frame, or multiple frames as the one constructed here.

Lay out the solar cells in your frame

Now you can lay out your strings of connected solar cells in the frame. For a permanent, heat resistant connection to the back board, use a glob of automotive gasket making silicone on the bottom of each cell. You can ask for this at any car parts store. Just ask for silicone gasket maker. Experimentation has shown that the double sided tape will not hold the cells properly in place when put in use. The solar panels get very hot during a normal day in the sun; therefore, they are only used to assist in moving the strings of cells as a single unit.

Notice that the layout here may vary from your own. How the cells are laid out does not matter as long as they are all together in series from plus to minus, plus, minus and so on. Be very careful when handling your cells as they break very easily.

If you break a solar cell anywhere in the process, simply remove it by first carefully using your soldering iron to heat the tabbing wire on the solar cell and then gently pry it up with a knife edge. When you have the tabbing wire removed from both sides of the broken solar cell, you can now replace it with a new cell.

You will probably break a cell or two in the process. I sure did. If you only chip off a corner or crack it a little, do not worry. It does not affect the performance of the overall solar panel too drastically. But, if you break off a larger portion of a solar cell, then you should remove that cell.

Note: Do not try to use hot glue or double sided tape to hold the solar cells to the frame. Many websites and DIY solar panel makers suggest using these items. We have tested both and they will fail due to heat from the sun.

Automotive silicone is designed for extremes of heat and cold and will last much longer. The DIY World test panel is still working well after 3 years outside.

Connecting the bus bars

In the picture above you see the bus bars connecting the rows of solar cells. Connect all of your cells in a series, remember plus to minus, to plus, to minus and so on.

On the top right side of the previous image you can see that both tabbing wires have been connected on the end of the last cell together. Then another piece of tabbing wire is run along to the center set of solar cells and connected to both of the tabbing wires sticking out of it.

Connect to the outside of your solar panel

Parts needed to connect to outside of panel.

Now you can gather together all the parts needed to connect your solar panel to the outside world. For this, it is best to use stainless steel bolts, nuts and washers for weather resistance and durability. The eye connectors are made of gold for long life. Stainless steel can also be used but are hard to find.

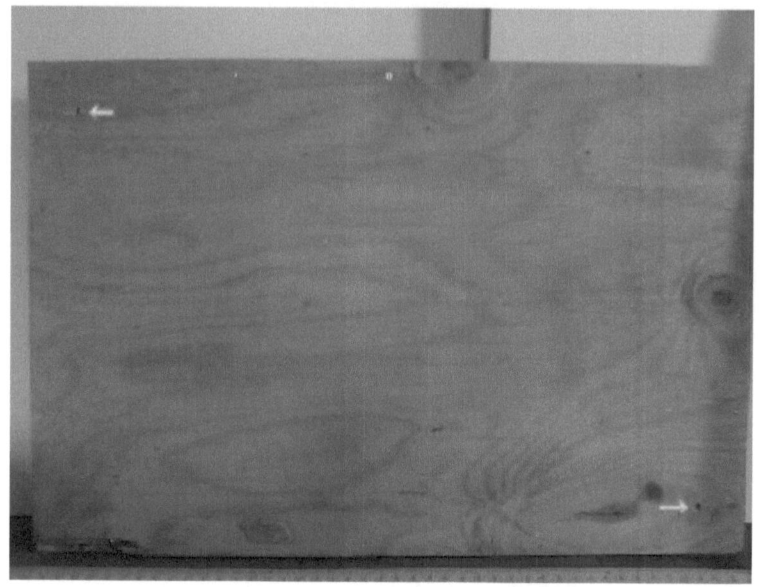

Drill holes for the outside connectors.

Next to the end terminals, both plus and minus ends, you will need to drill holes through the back board in order to connect the terminals from the solar panel to the outside. Look at both the above and the following photos for reference.

Hooking up the bus bar to an eye connector

At each end of your solar panel you will need to connect a bus bar. See the above picture for an example. The last two positive terminals should be connected together and soldered onto an eye connector. Then do the same with the two negative terminal ends. Make sure to line up the eye connectors with the holes that you just prepared.

Finished assembling the solar panel.

In the previous photo you can see the nearly completed solar panel. See how the bus bars connect each row of cells to the next, in series. Note also the two end terminals, both plus and minus with their eye connectors.

Note: At this point, if you wish, you may encapsulate your solar cells. This is an extra step that is not necessary, but will greatly extend the life of your solar panel. If you are interested in encapsulating your solar panel, please refer to the website:

http://www.thediyworld.com/DIY-Solar-Panels-How-To-Make-Your-Own.html

for videos and details

Repeat all the above steps

If you are making more than one solar panel, then repeat everything previously shown in order to make the solar panels exactly the same.

Test your solar panel

Use a voltmeter and test your solar panel. A digital meter is best used here because it is more forgiving if you hook it up backwards.

You should read about 17 - 18 volts per panel with a volt meter placed between the terminals of a solar panel out in full sunlight. If the voltage of any panel is less than 17 volts in full sunlight, then you need to check your connections between individual solar cells. This can be done by placing one lead of the volt meter on an output terminal and checking the end of each cell in a row until you find one that is not connected properly.

Re-solder the bad connection and test it all again for proper voltage.

Part three of the project – Make the plexiglass cover

In the following steps, you must be very careful again when working. Plexiglass can be quite tough, but it is very fragile when you are cutting it. It can snap, crack or break in bad angles as you work. Once the cutting is finished the stuff is very rugged and durable.

If your budget permits, you may be using solar glass or safety glass here instead of plexiglass. In this case, you may skip ahead to the next section. But remember that you will need a metal frame on top of your glass to hold it in place.

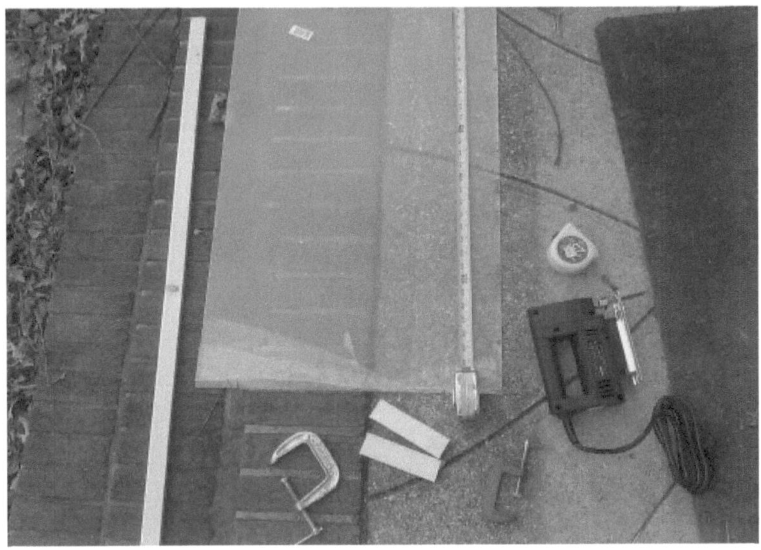

Laying out the tools to cut plexiglass

Make sure you get UV resistant plexiglass. Also get the thickest that you can afford. The thicker it is, the stronger it will be. Remember, this is supposed to endure the elements and, in some cases, the occasional tree branches or hail stones that fall on it.

There are special plexiglass cutting tools that you can purchase at the local hardware store. You score the plexiglass along the line you want to cut and then hold it firmly along a straight table edge and gently snap it apart along the scored lines. This may be a bit tricky, and, if you are not careful, the plexiglass may break at an odd angle. Through experimentation, it has been found that a Dremel with cutting tool works the best. It is easy to use and makes a clean cut. Actually, if you score it deeply on both sides, you may be able to break it evenly against a straight edge, but it is possible to crack a panel in this way. The best thing to do is cut it almost through. Use a slower setting to avoid burning too much.

Making a straight edge for cutting

No matter what method you choose to cut the plexiglass, simply measure it out to fit exactly over the frame of your solar panel and cut it.

Use wood and “C” clamps to make a straight edge for cutting

In the above photo, you can see that a “C” clamp and a couple pieces of wood have been used to make a straight edge on both sides of the plexiglass for cutting. Be sure to use wood on both sides of the “C” clamp in order to prevent damage to the plexiglass. Also, do not tighten the clamps too much or you may crack the plexiglass.

Notice, too, that the protective film has been left on the plexiglass for this step. This ensures that the plexiglass will not be scratched.

Drill holes through the panel to prepare for screws

Tack the plexiglass cover in place on your solar panel frame with a few drops of silicone sealer. This will make pre-drilling easier.

Take a drill bit just smaller than the screws you want to use. Pre-drill holes in each position that you want to place a screw in. You will want to use at least 4 or 5 screws per side for the best seal.

Drill just a little bit into the wood, as well, to make the screws go through easier.

Now take a drill bit that is just a tiny bit larger than the diameter of your screws. Drill through all the holes in the plexiglass, so there is no stress on it when you insert the screws. A screw should fit right through the plexiglass with ease. Do not drill out the wood frame with the larger drill bit, just the plexiglass. This will keep the plexiglass from cracking or splitting when you assemble the frame.

Holes pre-drilled for the mounting screws.

Note: It is strongly recommended that you use some sort of metal frame over the top, outside edges of your plexiglass. With time, the plexiglass will warp from the heat of the sun radiating on your solar panel. This will break the silicone seal and allow water inside your solar panel.

Our example does not show metal framework, but experience has shown it is very important to prevent water damage to your solar panel.

The arrows above show holes through plexiglass

You can put a couple screws in the frame to hold the work together and keep it straight as you go. These will need to be removed for the next step, but may help for now.

Get a tube of outdoor silicone sealer. Put your plexiglass sheets aside for now (remove any screws you may have used to hold it in place). Form a generous bead all around the outside edges of the solar panel frame. Keep it in the middle of each board for the best seal.

Now, carefully align the plexiglass cover on your frame and press down lightly all around to seal the silicone. You may want to insert a couple screws to help align the plexiglass. Now you can insert all your screws into the pre-drilled holes.

For an extra good seal, run a bead of silicone all around the outside edges of the plexiglass where it comes in contact with the wood frame. Use your finger (with a glove on) and smooth in the silicone to form a good seal.

Now you have finished the construction of your solar panel. If you are making more than one solar panel, do the same with the second panel and then proceed to the next step.

Solar panel completed

Part Four of the Project – Electrical Connections

Connecting the solar panels together

Note: this step is only for those who divide their solar panel into two smaller panels.

Cut a piece of 12 gauge or thicker wire long enough to connect between one of the positive terminals of one panel to a negative terminal of the other panel. This can easily be found with a multimeter. Simply measure the voltage and mark the terminals as plus or minus.

Use stainless steel (or gold) crimp connectors on each end of the wire and screw it down between the two solar panels, plus to minus. This connects them in series with each other, doubling the voltage to the desired total system voltage. It should be 18 volts or so in full sunlight. You can measure the total voltage by connecting a volt meter between the two remaining terminals of your solar panels.

In the following image you can see that the two panels have been connected together with a piece of scrap wood. This makes it easier to transport the panels as a single unit.

You can also see the connection between the two panels, connecting them in series. Notice the + and – markings on the photo below. One panel has been rotated around 180 degrees in order to have both a plus and a minus output at the bottom for ease of connecting wires to the outside world later on. The center plus and minus leads are connected together.

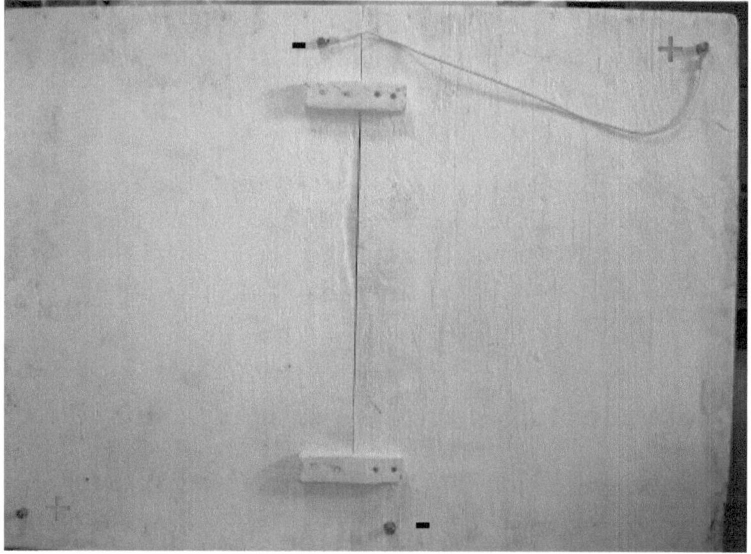

Take your solar panel outside

Take your new solar panel outside on a sunny day and angle it to face the sun for the final test. Hook up a volt meter between the plus and minus leads of your solar panel and measure the voltage. It should read somewhere between 17 – 18 volts DC.

If you do not get 18 volts, or close to it, in full sunlight, then something is wrong and you need to check the wiring of your solar panel. Make sure the crimp connectors are snug on the wire ends and that the screw terminals are tight.

Measuring the voltage of the finished solar panels

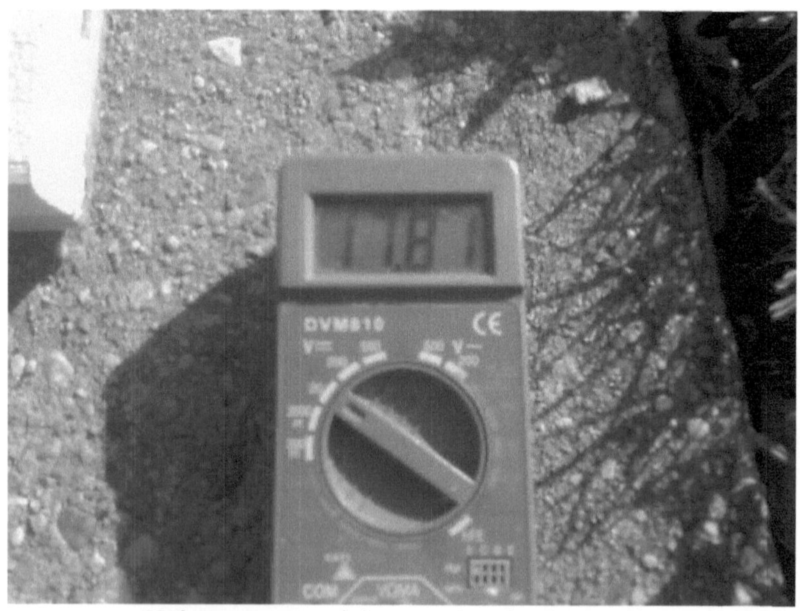

Voltage output of the completed solar panels

In the previous two photos you can see the completed solar panels lying out in the late afternoon sun. The panels are not angled properly to catch the sun's rays well. This was just to test the panel output. The voltage reads 17.81 volts, which shows us that the solar panels are working well. In indirect sunlight, they will put out just slightly under 18 volts.

Hooking up solar charge controller

Earlier in this book, solar charge controllers and their purpose were mentioned. Now you will hook up your solar charge controller to the solar panels and the battery bank.

Your solar charge controller will probably look a bit different than the one shown here, but they all have basically the same connections. There is a plus and minus input from the solar panel. There is a plus and minus output to the battery. And there is a plus and minus output to your load. The load is whatever device that you want to run with your solar powered system, such as a light bulb for example.

Make sure, when purchasing a solar charge controller, that it does have these three types of connections. You want to have the load output controlled by the charge controller in order to prevent damage to the batteries. The charge controller will disconnect your load (light bulb, television, etc) if the battery gets too low. Some cheap charge controllers may not have the load connections. Be sure not to get those.

Again, this is a budget DIY project. You may have a more expensive solar charge controller for your own project. It should not matter. Most connections are the same anyway.

Solar charge controller with the cover off

In the above photo you can see a common solar charge controller with the cover removed to show the connections. Notice the first two screws have the word “panel” under them. This is the connector for the solar panel.

The next two screws are labeled “battery”. This is where you hook up the battery or batteries.

The last pair of screws is labeled “load”. This is the output of the system. Here you can connect to the outside world to power lights, televisions and more.

This will be step by step from here on out.

Now, pull out your crimp on end connectors and a wire crimping tool. Any automotive store carries these.

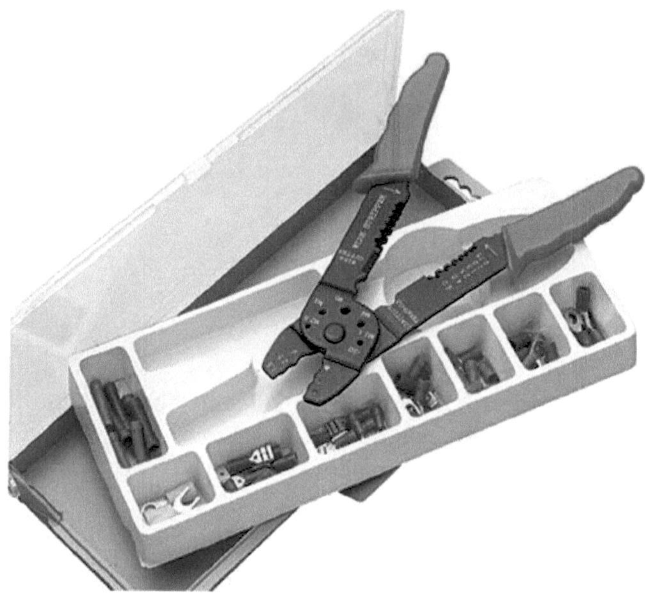

Standard automotive wire crimping set

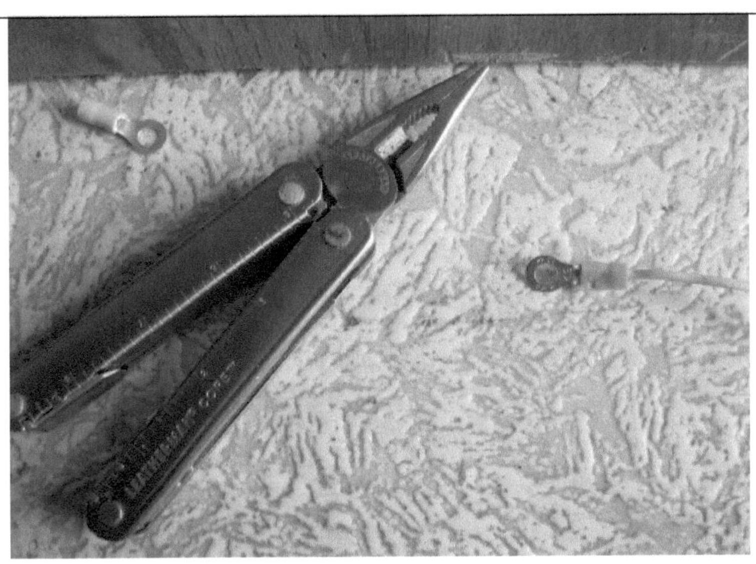

Crimp on end connectors and a Leatherman

For this job, a good old Leatherman was used. It has wire cutters, strippers and a wire crimping tool just like the automotive wire crimping tool in the previous photo.

Place your battery in a safe and well ventilated area. Explosive gasses can be given off during normal use of a lead acid battery, so it should always be well ventilated. Outdoors, in a garage or basement, or near a window is fine. If you can, set up a small 12 volt fan, such as a computer cooling fan, to keep air flowing around the battery if there is not enough natural air flow around it. Keep the battery off the floor with a piece of wood or plastic to protect it.

Find a good location nearby for your electrical connections. A wall just above the battery bank will do.

First, mount your solar charge controller to the wall with the provided screws. You will normally need to remove the cover to do this.

Cut a piece of wire long enough to reach from the battery positive terminal to the positive battery connector on your solar charge controller. Allow enough extra wire for error.

Now, depending on your particular battery and the available connections on top, the next step may vary. Most deep cycle batteries have a screw-on terminal and a normal round post terminal. The screw on terminal will be shown in this project.

You need to find ring type crimp-on end connectors that have a large enough ring to fit your battery screw terminal.

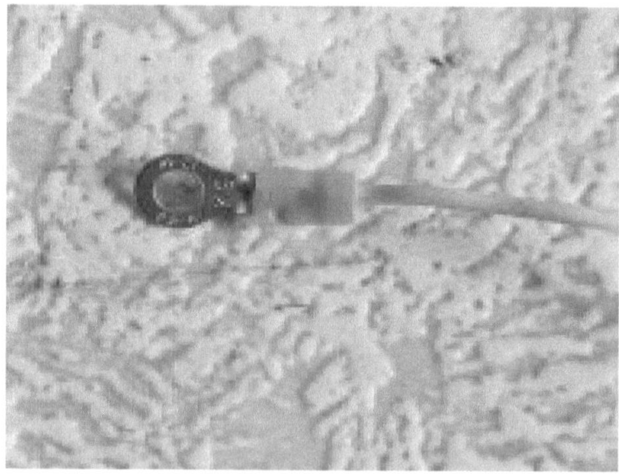

Strip off the end of a piece of wire about ¼ inch long and insert it into the end of the ring terminal.

Now use the wire crimping tool to crush it tightly around the wire.

Make sure the wire is set solidly into the terminal.

See the photo above. Notice the crushed area on the yellow part.

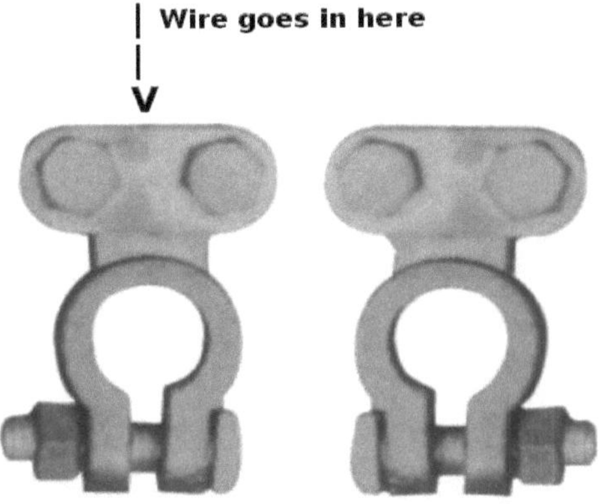

If your battery does not have screw-on terminals, but only posts, then you will need automotive battery terminals.

Screw the terminal onto the battery and tighten the bolt on the side. Next, insert your wire into the wire holder and tighten both screws down to fasten the wire to the battery.

Now on to the other end of the wire. Strip off ¼ inch from the end and insert it into the positive terminal post on your solar charge controller. You will need a screw driver to loosen the screw enough to get the wire in. While holding the wire in place with one hand, tighten the screw down onto the wire until it is secure.

Repeat this process for the negative terminal of the battery and the charge controller.

Both battery terminals are connected to the charge controller.

In this example, the battery is connected to a camper and is hooked up using battery clamps for quick connect and disconnect. You can see the battery in the next photo.

Deep cycle battery with battery clamps connected to solar charge controller.

No matter which method you use to connect the battery, be careful not to connect the terminals incorrectly. You may damage the solar charge controller if you do. Use two different colored wires to be safe.

The next step will be hard to show on a single photo. You are now able to connect the solar panel to the solar charge controller. The solar panel should be placed on the roof of your home, RV or outside in the sun. No matter where you place the solar panel, be sure to tilt it at about a 30 degree angle, and facing south, where it will catch the most sunlight during the day time.

The south facing, sloping roof top of your home is perfect. On the flat roof of an RV or camper works as well.

Get a pair of wires that reaches from your solar panel to your solar charge controller. Crimp on gold, or stainless steel, ring connectors to the ends of the wires that connect to the solar panel outside. Again, using different colored wires helps here a lot.

Run the wires down to your solar charge controller. This will vary based on your own personal setup. Strip off ¼ inch of plastic insulation from each wire and screw them into the appropriate terminals of the charge controller. Be sure to put the positive wire into the plus screw on the controller and the negative wire into the minus screw on the controller.

Solar panels and battery connected to charge controller.

In the photo above, you can now see an LED is lit up showing that the battery has been connected to the charge controller. Now the battery and the solar panels have been connected. All that remains is to connect the load.

The load is anything that you want to run off your solar power system. This can include a light, television, computer or anything else you can imagine. Just remember to watch the power ratings of the item you connect to the system. Power ratings will be discussed again later, so don't worry yet.

It is best to use a fuse box to protect the system from an accidental overload, or short circuit. In this way, you can prevent the possibility of a fire if something shorts out. The fuse will blow and protect the system from overloading. With no fuse, the battery is capable of providing enough power to melt your wires in seconds and could start a fire.

You can find an inline fuse at automotive stores or a fuse block at most electronics supply stores.

Connect the positive terminal of the solar charge controller “load” output to one side of the fuse block and the negative side of the “load” output directly to the item you are powering. This can be either a 12 volt device or a power inverter.

Connect the other side of the fuse block to the positive terminal of the device you are running.

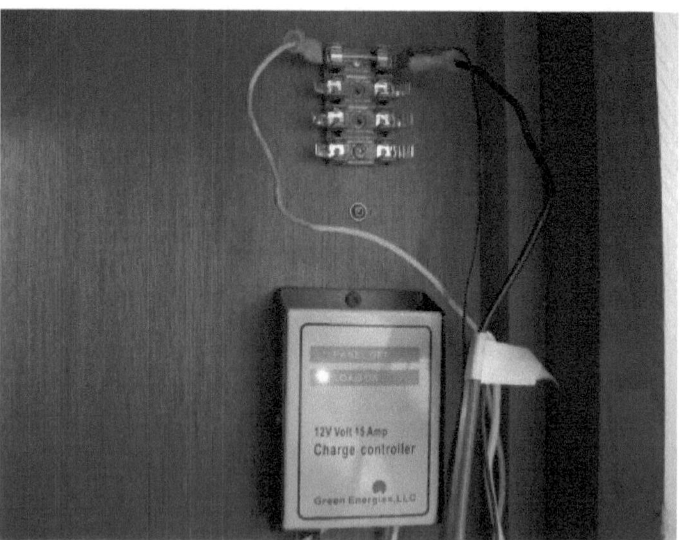

In the above photos, you can see the solar charge controller on the left with its cover off and all leads are connected to the terminals. On the right side, you can see the charge controller with its cover back in place and the fuse block which is connected to the "load" output of the charge controller. In this case, the load is a set of 12 volt LED lamps in a camper.

You can also connect a power inverter directly to the load output of the inverter in order to power 120 volt appliances. There are many types of power inverters on the market. Most of them either have a 12 volt cigarette lighter connector attached, or a pair of battery clamps. Another type is the grid tie inverter. If you choose the grid tie inverter, please see an electrician to safely connect it to your home.

Depending on your personal preference, there are two ways to go here.

You can buy the inverter with screw on terminals (on back left of image).

With this version, you can use some ring type crimp-on adapters and wire it directly into your solar charge controller. The original wires that come with it will not be used and can be set aside.

Or, you can get the type with a cigarette lighter plug attached. With this model, you will need to attach a cigarette lighter socket to your charge controller output in order to use the inverter.

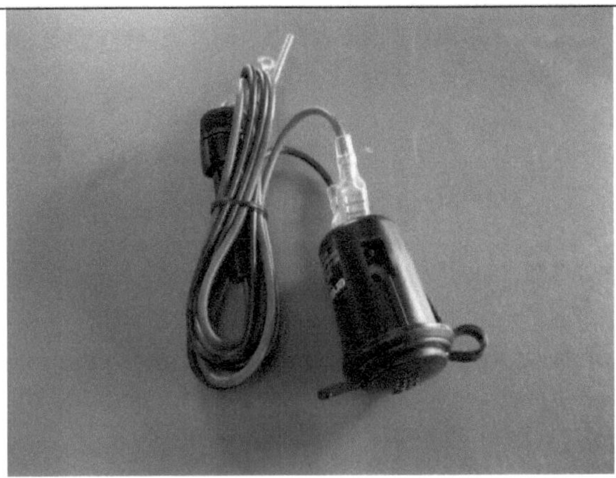

If you choose to use a cigarette lighter socket, you can connect the leads directly into the “load” output of the solar charge controller.

The sockets come with an inline fuse for protection, so you will not need a fuse block.

Next, you can plug your inverter into the socket to power appliances.

Part Five – Using Your Solar Power System

General Maintenance

Now that you have your solar panel and control circuitry set up, there are a few things you should know about using and maintaining your new solar power system.

The solar panels are normally rated to give you about 20 years of good, reliable service. Many last much longer, but with time, the amount of energy output will be reduced as the solar cells age.

After a heavy snow storm, your panels may need to be swept free of snow so that they can continue working.

Make sure that tree branches and leaves do not accumulate on top of your solar panels.

If you find that your panels are not operating at top outputs anymore, you should check all solder joints to make sure that none of them have separated. Extreme temperatures are formed inside your solar panel housing during the day time. Expansion and contraction of the solder joints may, with time, cause them to separate.

If you made the solar panels with a wood frame, make sure it is always well painted and periodically check the silicone seal to be sure it is water tight.

Battery Maintenance

Your batteries require monthly maintenance and supervision. Make sure that the battery compartment is well ventilated. As the batteries get charged, they give off explosive hydrogen gas. If not ventilated, this can be an explosion hazard. This gas is actually from the water being evaporated off. The water levels in the batteries will slowly go down and need to be refilled. Check your batteries monthly and top off the water levels, as needed, with distilled water. Do not use normal tap water or you will ruin your batteries. If your batteries are not maintenance free, which means sealed, then you can pry off the lids to see inside the battery cells. You should see a plastic ledge on most batteries which should be covered with water. If you can see the exposed plastic ledge, then slowly add distilled water until it is covered again. Do this for all the cells of all your batteries. Then carefully clean off the top of the battery with a mixture of water and baking soda, to neutralize any acid that may have spilled, and replace the covers.

Your batteries should last about 3 to 7 years, or more, depending on their type and quality and the conditions they are used in. Excessive deep discharging (below 10.5 volts) or over charging, and excesses of heat and cold, can affect your battery service life.

If your batteries are no longer capable of providing their full energy output, then it is time to replace them.

Using Your Solar Power

When using your solar power system, you should be aware of a few important things.

First, you need to keep your daily power usage in the range of your battery banks, or you will soon run out of power. If you have two 100Ah batteries, for example, then you have a total of 200 Amp Hours of usable energy at any given time. To convert this to how many watts you have, multiply 200 Ah by 12 Volts, and you get 2,400 Watts total reserve capacity in your batteries.

This may sound like a lot, but plug in a fridge and you will use about 1,000 Watts per day on average. Turn on a 100 Watt light bulb for 10 hours, and you use another 1,000 watts.

You should also match your batteries to your solar panels. It will not do you any good to have 2,000 watts of solar panels if the battery bank cannot take all that power. Likewise, be sure that the solar charge controller can handle the current put out by the solar panels. A 2,000 watt solar panel setup will be putting out about 167 Amps of power when the sun is shining. That is a lot of current. You would need a solar charge controller rated for that much current.

An average battery bank rated at 200 Ah can only take about 10 Amps of charging current at any given time, to be on the safe side. This means that you will need about seventeen 200 Ah batteries to handle all of that incoming energy. That is a lot of batteries.

Let's use a smaller, more attainable, example. If you have about 600 Watts of solar panels, then you have about 600 Watt Hours of usable energy every hour that the sun is shining. That means you will have 50 Amps of current coming into your batteries. You need a 50 Amp charge controller to handle that current. 600 Watts divided by 12

Volts = 50 Amps.

Now, assume that you have about 10 good sunny hours per day. That gives you a total of 6,000 usable Watts per day. 600 Watts for 10 hours = 6,000 Watts.

To calculate how many Ah of battery capacity you need, divide your total daily Watts by 12 Volts. 6,000 Watts divided by 12 Volts = 500 Ah. You need a total battery capacity of 500 Amp Hours.

However, things are not that simple. Now, remember that a battery has a C20 rating. This means that the battery is rated at how many Amps it can sustain for 20 hours. You should only discharge your batteries to about 50%, and batteries should be charged according to their C20 rating. 500Ah divided by 20 hours = 25 Amps of charging current. Since, in this example, there is a total of 50 Amps coming in, you need to double the battery capacity to be able to handle that much power. You need about 1,000 Ah battery capacity.

So, for a 600 Watt solar panel, you would need a 50 Amp solar charge controller and about five 200 Amp Hour batteries.

Calculating how much energy you can use at any given time is simple since we already did the math above. You can safely draw from a battery at its C20 rating. With 1,000 Ah of battery capacity, divide by 20 and you get 50 Amps. 50 x 12 volts = 600 Watts of energy. You would need a 600 Watt power inverter if you wanted to draw this much energy from your solar power setup.

Appendix A – Terms and Definitions

Amp Hour (AH) – Amp Hours are the amount of hours that a lead acid battery can maintain a constant load of 20 Amps. For example, a 100 AH battery can maintain 100 Amps for one hour or 1 Amp for 100 hours. The same battery can maintain a 20 Amp load for 5 hours.

Battery Bank – One or more lead acid batteries connected together to provide more total output for your solar energy system.

C20 Rating – A battery has a C20 rating, which is a calculation of how many amps it can put out over a 20 hour period. For example, a 100Ah battery has a C20 rating of 5 Amps. This battery can sustain a drain of 5 Amps for 20 hours.

Inverter or Power Inverter – This is a device that converts the 12 volt energy from a battery bank to 120 volts for household appliances.

Parallel Connections – You can connect two or more batteries together in parallel to add up their total usable current (Amps). Two 12 Volt, 100 AH batteries connected together in parallel gives you a total of 200 AH capacity, but the voltage stays the same.

Series Connections – When electronic devices are connected in series, they are connected from plus to minus, to plus to minus, and so on. On one end is a positive lead and on the other is a negative lead. When devices are connected in series, the voltages are all added together, but current stays the same. For example, if you connect two 6 Volt batteries in series, then you get a total of 12 Volts. You will be connecting solar cells in series to get a total of 18 Volts out.

Solar Charge Controller – This is a device that monitors the state of charge of your batteries and can disconnect the solar panels from the batteries to prevent overcharging. The charge controller can also disconnect the load (devices you are powering) from the batteries to prevent damage from deep discharging.

Watt Hour (WH) – Watt Hours is a measurement of how long your solar power system can sustain a draw of a certain amount of Watts. For example, if you have a total capacity of 100 WH, and are using a 100 Watt light bulb, then you can run the light for one hour. Or, if you use a 10 Watt lamp, you can run it for 10 hours.

Appendix B – Finding Solar Cells and Materials

Purchasing Solar Cells

Solar cells can be found, most inexpensively, on the internet. Do a web search for "cheap solar cells" or use an online auction site to find the best deals. Buying in bulk will be much cheaper per watt than buying smaller quantities.

Solar cells are also graded according to manufacturing quality. Grade A will be near perfect, and have no visible flaws, but will cost more. Grade B will have small imperfections, or chipped edges, and will be much cheaper. Broken solar cells are the cheapest per watt. You can find broken solar cells by the pound online. Ebay is one of the largest sources of affordable solar cells. Broken cells are still usable and each piece puts out energy relative to its surface area. Half a solar cell will put out half of the total energy that the whole solar cell would.

One important point to remember when using broken solar cells is that the total amount of energy produced by the solar panel is limited by the smallest piece. Because of this, try to keep all of your broken solar cells relatively the same size in a solar panel.

Solar Panel Backing Material

For backing material in your solar panel, you can use wood, metal or plastic. Wood is the cheapest but will need to be painted well to weatherproof it. Wood will also need to be repainted every couple years to keep your solar panel in good shape.

When choosing a backing material, look for a sturdy, rigid material to protect your fragile solar cells inside the solar panel.

Solar Glass, Plexiglass or Safety Glass

For the protective cover of your solar panel, you must use a rigid, clear material such as glass. The cover must be able to withstand hail storms, UV rays, rain and snow. The best option is solar glass, which is specially made for solar panels. It is also the most expensive.

You can use safety glass as well. Standard glass may break if hit with hail stones, so it should be avoided.

Plexiglass can be used, if you find the ultra violet resistant plexiglass. When using plexiglass, you will also have heat issues over time. The inside of a solar panel will be very hot in the sun, which may cause warping of your plexiglass. A metal rim or frame around the top of your solar panel is strongly advised in order to prevent warping that will break the seal around your frame and allow water into your solar panel.

Solar cell Encapsulant

Encapsulating your solar cells will protect them from the elements and help keep them from cracking under stress. This is optional and costly but will greatly extend the life of your solar panel.

Solar encapsulant comes in two forms. One form is a silicone elastomer that can be spread on top of your solar cells. When cured, it forms a protective layer. This is the most expensive form, but it is easy to work with.

Another form is an EVA sheet, which is a flexible, rubbery type of material. You lay a sheet of this material over your solar cells and use a heat gun, or hot hair dryer, to heat shrink the material into your solar cells. This form is cheaper, at about $20 per square yard of material, online.

Either one of these methods forms a permanent, protective barrier over the top of your solar cells and extends the life of your solar panel.

It is admirable that you have chosen to take on a project such as this one, incorporating environmental improvements with a money-saving technique. Whether this is your first attempt in the realm of Do-It-Yourself, or you have an extensive background in it, we at The DIY World hope that this book has been helpful.

Questions, comments and concerns are always welcome.

You can post your comments in our forum at:
http://www.thediyworld.com/forum

Have fun and good luck!

www.ingramcontent.com/pod-product-compliance
Ingram Content Group UK Ltd.
Pitfield, Milton Keynes, MK11 3LW, UK
UKHW041925190726
13854UKWH00003B/1455